TEXAS POLITICS IN THE GILDED A
GE, 1873-1890

WINTZ, CARY D. 1943-

F391.W748 1983

SC

**SOUTH CAMPUS LIBRARY
TARRANT COUNTY COLLEGE
5301 CAMPUS DRIVE
FORT WORTH, TEXAS 76119**

Texas Politics in the Gilded Age, 1873-1890

Cary D. Wintz

AMERICAN PRESS
Boston, Massachusetts

Cover photo: Courtesy of Barker Texas History Center Photograph Collection.

Copyright © 1983 by American Press.

All rights reserved. No part of this publication may be reproduced, stored in a retrieval system, or transmitted, in any form or by any means, electronic, mechanical, photocopying, recording, or otherwise, without the prior written permission of the copyright owner.

Printed in the United States of America.

Preface

The TEXAS HISTORY SERIES of American Press consists of original essays about Texas history written primarily for undergraduates. The series examines a wide variety of topics, some traditional such as Hispanic colonization, the Texas Revolution, or Reconstruction; others address topics that are usually minimized or ignored such as women in Texas, organized labor, or cultural diversity.

The series will be topically complete for courses in Texas History. It has no limits. Instead, it will be continually added to in response to new research and as gaps in our list are identified. This approach will keep the list current and fresh, and its freshness will be enhanced by our technology which permits authors to make changes in their published essays as needed.

Each essay may be purchased separately, allowing professors to choose those essays appropriate to their specific courses and emphases. The cost of each book has been kept very low. This series makes it possible to select a topically complete and well organized set of books at a total cost very competitive with the inflexible textbooks currently available. Several essays may even be bound into one volume and provide additional savings for your students without compromising the quality of your course.

The TEXAS HISTORY SERIES is designed to offer the freshest possible course materials in a format that permits flexibility for instructors and economy for students. We believe it offers a unique alternative to standard texts.

ROBERT J. ROSENBAUM
Editor

Contents

Introduction 1

Richard Coke and the Emergence of the
  Conservative Democratic Coalition 5

Agrarian Dissent: Greenbackers, The Grange, and
  the Democratic Party 18

Wash Jones and the Independent Challenge to the
  Democratic Party 27

Democratic Unity Under Stress: Land Policy,
  Prohibition, and Railroad Regulation 37

The Collapse of the Conservative Democratic
  Coalition 49

Suggestions for Further Reading 61

Introduction

In the mid-1870s Democrats regained control of the Texas government following a brief period of military rule and several years during which Republicans had controlled the state. The new Democratic government was committed to eliminating the last traces of Republican power, reversing the policies of Reconstruction, and establishing an administration based on conservative principles and the concept of limited government. In the fifteen years following the election of Richard Coke in 1873, a succession of conservative Democrats occupied the governor's mansion and controlled most other state offices. The Republican Party, whose domination of the government had been tenuous at best, quickly shrank in influence and ceased to seriously challenge Democratic rule. For all practical purposes, Texas had become a one party state.

The resurgence of the Democratic Party did not mean that those who had run the state during the late 1850s had returned to power. Prior to the Civil War, planters had dominated Texas politics, and, as the war approached, the issues associated with plantations, slavery, and States' rights overshadowed traditional issues like land policy and protection of the frontier. During the 1860s many Texans were unable to participate in politics, first because they were away at war, and then because Reconstruction law disenfranchised them. In the 1870s Texans confronted new realities: they had lost the war, slavery had been abolished, and the planter class no longer dominated the state's economy or politics. Democrats were now the party of farmers, ranchers, railroad men, lawyers, and businessmen, while the political debates of the 1870s and 1880s focused on issues like land policy, the public debt, law and order, railroad regulation, and public education. The immediate objectives of the leadership of the Democratic Party were to establish firm control over the machinery of state government, cut government expenses and reduce the state debt, eradicate the last vestiges of Republican rule, and replace it with a solidly conservative government.

Texas Democrats met these objectives with little difficulty. Beginning in 1874 five Democratic governors anchored the conservative's domination of the state administration. The Republican Party, torn by internal divisions and further weakened by its identification in the public's mind as the party of Reconstruction, offered no real challenge to the Democrats. Third parties and independent candidates represented a more serious threat to conservative Democrats, but during the 1870s and 1880s conservatives adopted enough agrarian reform measures to undermine and divide their liberal opposition and retain control of the government.

Despite the overwhelming success of conservative Democrats at the polls, Texas was not as politically homogeneous as it appeared to be. The persistence of third party candidates and independents reflected the fact that a sizeable minority of Texans were dissatisfied with conservative rule. Several factors contributed to this. First, Texas was large and heterogeneous with potential divisions between various regions of the state, with conflicting economic interests, and with conflicting ethnic groups and religious denominations. Although agriculture dominated the state's economy throughout the nineteenth century, agricultural interests were quite diverse. By the 1880s the 37 percent of Texas farmers who were tenant farmers or sharecroppers had potential political differences with landowners, while farmers, cattlemen, and sheepherders sometimes competed for the same land

and often conflicted over issues like the tariff and land policy. As business and industry grew in the 1880s, agrarian interests became increasingly concerned about government regulation of railroads and anti-trust legislation. On the other hand manufacturers, lumbermen, merchants, and the railroads often disagreed about the tariff and railroad regulation.

Ethnic and religious differences also undermined political unity. By 1880 nearly two-thirds of the state's population were Anglo-Americans and native Southerners, most of whom were either Southern Baptists or Methodists. Members of these two denominations held similar religious and political views, overwhelmingly supported the Democratic Party, and controlled most state offices. The majority supported the concept of a conservative, limited government, although a significant number wanted the state to restrict the use of alcoholic beverages. In central Texas, several counties had a significant German population. Germans were usually Lutheran or Catholic, opposed prohibition, and divided almost evenly between Republicans and Democrats. In the counties south of the Nueces River, Mexicans and Mexican-Americans constituted either a majority or large minority of the population. This group was predominently Catholic, usually poor and economically dependent on Anglo-American employers, and often the victims of prejudice and hostility. Blacks formed the largest minority group in the state. While they constituted only about 25 percent of the total population, blacks were the majority in fourteen counties in the former plantation belt along the Brazos and Colorado Rivers and in East Texas, and large black minorities existed elsewhere. Most blacks were either Southern Baptists or Methodists, but, unlike their white counterparts, most supported the Republican Party, and very few endorsed prohibition. Like Mexican-Americans, many blacks were impoverished and suffered from discrimination.

Efforts of Democrats to bridge these differences were limited by the absence of strong party leadership and by the emergence of a number of political issues that threatened to further divide the party. The five governors who served from 1874 to 1891 seemed cut from a similar mold. All had been officers in the Confederate Army, all, except Lawrence Sullivan Ross, were attorneys, and while all were fairly competent administrators, none provided strong party or state leadership. Lacking a dominant political figure like Sam Houston, the Democrats of this period experienced several divisive squabbles over leadership. Also the major political issues worked against party unity. While there was a general consensus for limiting the role of government and reducing the state debt in the late 1870s, in the following decade issues like prohibition, land policy, and railroad regulation threatened to further divide the party.

Texas during the period betwen the end of Reconstruction and the 1890s was beginning to experience the economic and social changes that would lead to the rapid growth, industrialization, and urbanization that so radically transformed the state in the twentieth century. The conservative Democrats who held power during these years attempted to build a state political coalition during a time of impending change. Initially they maintained party unity by emphasizing the sins of Republican rule and Reconstruction; as the state became more diversified, this party unity would become increasingly difficult to sustain.

Richard Coke and the Emergence of the Conservative Democratic Coalition

Traditionally, the Democratic Party has dominated politics in Texas. Although the Democratic Party did not exist in Texas prior to annexation, the "Houston" and "anti-Houston" factions closely mirrored contemporary political parties in the United States. Sam Houston's policies were essentially those of the Jacksonian Democrats, while Mirabeau B. Lamar's anti-Houston party endorsed many of the programs associated with the Whig party. However, at the time of annexation most Texans identified with the Democrats, since that party had championed Texas' entry into the Union. The Whig Party, weakened in the late 1840s by the conflict over slavery, never effectively established itself as a force in Texas politics. In the mid-1850s, Texans who were uncomfortable with the Democrats found temporary refuge in the Know-Nothing or American Party, but generally returned to the Democratic fold with the collapse of that organization in 1857. The growing sectional crisis divided the Democrats into Unionist and States' Rights factions, but after secession most Unionists either supported the Confederacy, or attempted, with little success, to maintain a neutral position. After the Civil War the extension of the suffrage to blacks and the disenfranchisement of former Confederate leaders resulted in the temporary dominance of the Republican Party. By the early 1870s, however, Democrats had begun to regain political control. In 1871 the party won all four of the state's Congressional seats, and the following year they gained a majority in the Legislature. Then, in December 1873, the Democratic gubernatorial candidate, Richard Coke, out-polled the incumbent Republican governor, Edmund J. Davis, 85,549 to 42,633. Democrats once again controlled the state government.

In the mid-1870s, the Democratic Party differed from their Republican opponents over the issue of race, in their attitude toward state finances, and in their perception of the role of government. When they resumed power, Democrats reduced the number of blacks holding public office in the state, but because of the relatively low percentage of the black population in most counties, the party did not launch an all-out campaign to restrict black suffrage. In contrast to Republicans, Democrats did try to lower state spending, diminish the role of state government, and eliminate or severely reduce funding for a number of social programs installed by the more activist Davis administration. Reflecting the role that businessmen played in their party leadership, Democrats supported railroad and industrial development. However, because Texas was still a predominantly rural state, and because Texas farmers tended to be more highly organized than their counterparts in other Southern states, agrarian interests exercised significant influence in the party. In the mid-1870s, conflict between business and agricultural interests was minimal as the Democrats concentrated on unseating the Republicans and reversing policies introduced during Reconstruction.

The Republican Party, which was established in Texas just after the Civil War, counted some Texas unionists among its members, but its successes during the late 1860s were based largely on the black vote. As early as 1868, Texas Republicans had split into two factions. Andrew J. Hamilton, a former Texas Congressman who served in the Union Army and was appointed provisional governor of the state in June 1865, led the conservative wing of the party, while Edmund J. Davis, a Union Army brigadier general from Texas, headed the radical faction. The Republicans differed from the Democrats by more actively supporting civil rights, railroad and industrial

Texas Politics in the Gilded Age, 1873-1890

Barker Texas History Center Photograph Collection

Governor and U.S. Senator Richard Coke

development, and funding for public education. They also endorsed the concept of an active state government with a broad program of social services. Also, under Republican rule taxes increased and the state debt soared. Throughout the 1870s and 1880s blacks provided the party with the majority of its support, although a significant number of Mexican-Americans, and Germans, and even a few Anglos identified with the Republican cause.

The gubernatorial election of 1873 signaled the collapse of Republican rule and the end of Reconstruction in Texas. The Thirteenth Legislature, which convened in January 1873, was controlled by Democrats and began the process of limiting the power of Governor Davis. Among the legislation enacted was a law which set the next general elections in Texas for December 1873. Both parties held their nominating conventions late in the summer of that year. Republicans met in Dallas, renominated Governor Davis, condemned the efforts of the Democratic Legislature to undermine the Governor's programs, and endorsed an extensive series of social reforms. Democrats, meeting in Austin, nominated Richard Coke, praised the work of the Thirteenth Legislature, called for conservative and responsible government, and promised to convene a new constitutional convention. The election evoked strong passions on both sides; each party used fraud and intimidation to further its cause. The outcome, however, was not even close. Coke won by a two-to-one margin, while his party retained solid control over both houses of the legislature.

The December election did not end the conflict engendered by the campaign. Republicans charged that the 1873 election law, under which the December election was held, was invalid on the grounds that it had limited voting to only one day rather than the four days mandated by the Texas Constitution. When the Republican-controlled state Supreme Court ruled that the 1873 election law was unconstitutional, Governor Davis declared that the entire election was illegal, ordered that the new Governor and Legislature "not attempt to assume the positions they claim," and appealed to President Grant for federal troops to block the upcoming inauguration. On January 12, 1874, one day before the new Legislature was scheduled to convene, President Grant rejected Davis' appeal and urged him to accept the results of the recent election. Tensions mounted as the new Legislature occupied the capitol building and armed men from both parties confronted each other in the streets of Austin. Surrounded by bodyguards, Richard Coke took the oath of office late at night on January 15. Two days later, after repeated requests for federal assistance went unanswered, E. J. Davis surrendered the Governor's office.

Richard Coke brought to Austin a commitment to reduce both the expenses and the activities of government, and a determination to restore the laissez faire approach to government that had prevailed in Texas prior to the Civil War. Of particular concern was the desperate condition of the state's finances. When Coke took office the state treasury was empty, there were outstanding debts of over $2,000,000, and recent efforts to market $900,000 in state bonds in New York failed because no one was willing to invest in Texas securities. In addition, the state faced lawsuits from several disgruntled creditors. Coke approached these problems by cutting government spending, refinancing the state's short-term debt, and marketing new long-term bonds at higher interest rates. These efforts were fairly effective and the credit of the state improved, although the high interest paid on long-term bonds would defeat efforts to balance the budget and retire the state debt for several years. Also, Coke's attempt to reform the state's tax system in order to more accurately assess and collect taxes failed. Consequently, even with taxes set at the maximum rate allowed by the Constitution, tax revenue did not cover the expenses of government and the state was forced to rely on the sale of public land and on borrowing to raise enough funds to conduct its business.

Coke also had promised the voters of Texas that, if elected, he would eliminate all traces of the recent Republican administration. Shortly after taking office, Coke launched an attack on the Republican dominated state judicial system. A constitutional amendment approved in the December election expanded the size of the state Supreme Court from three to five members, and terminated the terms of the current justices. Coke consequently named five Democrats, including Chief Justice Oran M. Roberts, to the high bench. The Legislature then was flooded with resolutions seeking to remove Republican state district judges from office. The complaints levied against Republican magistrates ranged from the physical disability of some judges to outright malfeasance; specific charges included dereliction of duty, arbitrary decisions, legal incompetence, and political bias. This purge was quick and quite effective. By the middle of 1874 the most outspoken Republican judges had been replaced by conservative Democrats.

In 1875, Democrats turned their attention to the last vestige of Republican rule, the Constitution of 1869. While Democrats were virtually unanimous in their demand for a new constitution, Coke delayed action for almost two years because of the expense involved in convening a convention. However, after a legislative commission failed in its efforts to rewrite the Constitution, Coke called a special election and the voters of Texas selected delegates to a constitutional convention that would meet in Austin in September 1875. Objections to the existing Constitution centered on both the Republican origins of the document and a genuine concern about the nature of the government that it created. In general, many Texans favored a weaker government more responsible to the electorate. For example, they felt that state judges should be elected rather than appointed to office, and wanted to limit the terms of most elected officers to two years. The new Constitution was modeled on the original Texas state Constitution of 1845, which had centered power in the hands of Legislature which met biennially, weakened the authority of the Governor, and placed severe limits on the power of the state to tax and incur indebtedness.

The delegates who assembled in Austin on September 6, 1875 represented an interesting cross section of the state. An overwhelming majority were Democrats, while only fifteen, including six blacks, were Republican. Forty-one of the delegates were farmers and twenty-nine were lawyers. The San Antonio *Herald* questioned the overall ability of the delegates, but noted that there were a few very capable men in attendance. Included among the men of great ability were John H. Reagan, former postmaster general of the Confederacy and future United States Senator, future governor Lawrence Sullivan "Sul" Ross, and Thomas L. Nugent, a future leader of the People's Party in Texas. The Grange, a farmers' organization that had appeared in the state in 1873 and had quickly become an outspoken although fairly moderate voice of agrarian protest, controlled a block of at least forty votes at the convention, and exerted considerable influence on the nature of the new Constitution. Like a majority of Texans, the Grange favored reducing the power of government (especially by cutting expenditures and the state's power to tax or borrow funds), limiting funding for public education, prohibiting the state from chartering banks, and restricting the power of railroads and big business.

The Texas Constitution of 1876 encorporated many of the values voiced by the Grange. It severely restricted the power of government, partially out of a determination to insure that if Radical Republicans regained control of the state, the perceived abuses of Reconstruction could not be repeated, and partly out of the conviction that a limited government best served the interests of the people. Legislative power was vested in a bicameral body which met in biennial sessions, and state senators had their term of office cut from six to four years. More significantly, the Constitution prohibited the Legislature from incurring a debt of greater than $200,000 and placed a strict limit on the maximum allowable *ad valorem* tax rate. The Governor, whose term of office was reduced from four to two years, was given virtually no control over other elected executive officers. Reacting against the very unpopular judicial system put into place by the Radical Republicans, the new Constitution reduced the number of district judges and required that all state judges be elected to office and serve terms ranging from four to six years.

Despite efforts by the Grange, the new Constitution took only tentative steps toward railroad regulation. It did make it illegal for competing railroads to merge and it gave the Legislature the authority to exercise some control over railroad rates. It also empowered the Legislature to aid railroad construction through grants of public land rather than with state funds or bonds. However, it did not create a regulatory agency to police railroad activities or implement effective control over rail rates. The Constitution also provided grants of public land to supplement funding for public education. However, the section on education reduced the amount and value of public land that had been set aside in 1858 to fund the still unbuilt University of Texas, decentralized state control over public education by abolishing the office of the state superintendent of education, eliminated compulsory school attendance, reduced the overall tax support for education, and segregated the public schools. The effect of this was to drastically reduce the level of aid for education that had been provided by the Constitution of 1869. The Constitution of 1876 also placed limits on the tax rate that cities and towns could assess. The section on voting precipitated the most heated debate. Delegates turned back efforts to restrict black suffrage through the implementation of a poll tax, refused to extend women the right to vote, and abolished the requirement that voters must register. As a result the new Constitution continued the practice of universal manhood suffrage.

The final document produced by the Austin convention engendered neither enthusiastic support nor harsh criticism. Most of the delegates signed the Constitution; only eleven voted against it. After setting a February date for a general election to ratify the Constitution and elect new state officers, the convention adjourned on November 24, 1875.

In preparation for the upcoming elections both Republicans and Democrats scheduled state conventions in January 1876. At both gatherings the central issue was party unity. The Democrats unanimously renominated Governor Coke. Coke was colorful but politically astute, and successfully courted the support of a broad spectrum of Democrats by combining conservative retrenchment policies with rural progressivism while he endorsed railroad and business development. Potential opponents of the popular Coke lacked a candidate strong enough to challenge the Governor, and did not want needlessly to jeopardize party unity. The desire for party unity also prompted three early challengers to the renomination of Lieutenant Governor Richard B. Hubbard to withdraw from the race. The party adopted a platform that was vague enough to appeal to all of its members. They defended states' rights, called for greater protection for border settlements, and condemned the Republican administration in Washington. The Convention carefully avoided two divisive issues; they remained neutral in the debate over the ratification of the new state Constitution, and they refused to take a position on the Specie Resumption Act recently passed by Congress.

While the Democrats celebrated party harmony in Galveston, Republicans, meeting in Houston, faced serious internal division. The party had split into a conservative faction, led by Texas Republicans who held positions in the federal government, and the radicals, who counted on the support of most black voters, and who rallied around the former governor E. J. Davis. Since blacks made up about 90 percent of the party's strength, the Davis faction managed to maintain control of the convention. Despite their numerical significance, blacks held few positions of leadership in the party. Most of the nominees to state office, as well as the delegates to the national convention, presidential electors, and state committee members were white, Southern born, pre-Civil War migrants to Texas, about half of whom were Confederate veterans. When E. J. Davis turned down the gubernatorial nomination, the convention selected William M. Chambers, a Confederate veteran and former Republican district judge. All but one of the delegates chosen to represent Texas at the National Republican Convention were Davis men.

The Republican platform opposed the new state Constitution, principally on the grounds that it failed to adequately support public education. Republicans endorsed the Grant administration, called for strict enforcement of the anti-Klu Klux Klan laws, and condemned the economic and tax policies of the Coke administration.

The election of 1876 was one-sided. Democrats contrasted the economic conservatism of Governor Coke with the extravagance of the Davis administration. Chambers and other Republican candidates really did little campaigning. Newspapers overwhelmingly endorsed the Democratic ticket, and the voters gave Coke an even greater landslide than he had won three years earlier. Coke received 150,681 votes to only 47,719 for Chambers. Texans approved the Constitution by a somewhat smaller margin, 136,606 votes to 56,653. Republican votes came mainly from the counties with a black majority and from several Hill Country counties that had a sizeable German population.

The strength of the Democratic victory on the state level tended to mask divisions that were surfacing in the party which would have an effect on Texas politics during the next decade. In several local elections the regularly nominated Democratic candidates faced opposition from independent Democrats who often disagreed with the positions taken by the official nominees. This division of the party at the local level gave some Republican candidates a chance for victory; in other races independent Democrats persuaded black Republicans to join them in opposing the regular Democratic candidate. The unity which had prevailed at the state convention did not prevent conflict from erupting among diverse interest groups at the local level.

Even the party's unified support of Richard Coke did not last long after the election. One of the first duties of the new Legislature was to select a United States Senator to replace the Republican incumbent, Morgan C. Hamilton. For several years newspapers had speculated about the potential candidacy of several prominent Democrats, but when the Legislature convened, attention focused on three front-runners, Governor Coke, Congressman John Hancock, and former Supreme Court Justice John Ireland. As the race intensified, the party unity, so evident in January, began to fade. Governor Coke jumped to an early lead. His popularity as governor and his connections with the Grange made him the man to beat. Hancock, who had opposed secession, drew support from former unionists and Hill Country Germans, and was the candidate most acceptable to the Republicans. Ireland's strength came from the area around his home in South Texas, and from East Texas where his integrity and Civil War record won him the endorsement of former planters.

Coke had to overcome a surprising amount of criticism in his quest for the Senate seat. Some objected to his giving up the Governor's office so soon after election, while others found fault with his failure to live up to his campaign promises—especially his promise to reduce the state debt. On the other hand Hancock's unionism proved to be more of a handicap than a benefit as critics insisted that a unionist could not adequately represent the people of Texas. Ireland had to contend with newspaper charges that he was involved in a conflict of interest related to railroad construction and that he had opposed the new state Constitution. More importantly, Ireland, who was acknowledged to be a "true Southern gentleman," seemed too impractical and too wedded to the ante-bellum past. Although the Legislature took several ballots to reach a decision, Coke prevailed, largely because he symbolized the resurgence of the Democratic Party in Texas, because of his strong support among farmers, and because he ultimately appeared more moderate and more responsible than either of his opponents.

Although he was elected to the Senate in May 1876, Coke did not resign the Governor's office until the following March, when Hamilton's term of office actually expired. At this time Lieutenant Governor Richard Hubbard became the state's chief executive. During the nearly two years that he served as Governor, no significant policy changes occurred. One reason for this was that except for the final weeks of the Fifteenth Legislature, which was still in session when Coke's resignation took effect, Hubbard served during a period when the Legislature did not meet. The new Governor did commit himself to cutting government expenses and reducing the state debt, but he was unable to meet this goal. Despite his efforts the state budget continued to run a deficit and the state debt steadily increased.

The divisions in both political parties that had surfaced in 1875 and early 1876 were reflected in the national elections the following Fall. The Republican delegation to the National Convention was dominated by the radical wing of the party and led by former Governor Davis. While they were more concerned about civil rights than economic issues, Davis did endorse the Specie Resumption Act. Texas Republicans initially endorsed the presidential candidacy of A. B. Norton, a radical from Indiana, but eventually switched to Rutherford B. Hayes. Davis' selection as a national committeeman insured his continuing control of the party in Texas for the next several years. At the Democratic Convention, the Specie Resumption Act was the major issue. Agricultural interests from the South and West feared that the act, which would place the nation on the gold standard by January 1879, would deflate prices, reduce farm income, and make it increasingly difficult for debtors to repay their obligations. While most Southern and Western Democrats called for the repeal of the act, the Texas delegation, optimistic about the party's chances for victory and therefore anxious to promote party unity, supported a compromise plank that merely sought to delay the implementation of the law. Texans also backed the nomination of Samuel J. Tilden. In the general election Tilden easily outpolled Hayes in Texas 106,382 to 45,013.

The most interesting local race in the November elections occurred in the Fifth Congressional District of South Central Texas. By 1874 all six of the state's Congressmen were Democrats who agreed on most major issues. They favored federal appropriations for river and harbor improvements in the state, the transfer of federal troops from other parts of the South to the Texas frontier, and lowering the protective tariff. However, the Texas delegation split over the currency issue, with four favoring the repeal of the Specie Resumption Act, while two, including John Hancock supported the measure. With the exception of Hancock, each incumbent received the party's nomination and easily defeated his Republican opponent. Hancock, whose political position had been undermined by his unsuccessful bid for the Senate seat and his unpopular stand on the currency issue, lost the nomination to Brenham banker D. C. Giddings. Then George W. "Wash"

Jones, a former unionist who had served with distinction in the Confederate army, and as the Democratic Lieutenant Governor in the Throckmorton administration, stunned the party by announcing that he would challenge Giddings as an independent candidate. The popular Jones ran a strong race, attacking his opponent for alleged impropriety in the marketing of state bonds, and drawing support from small farmers (landowners and tenants), black Republicans, and Democratic unionists. Although Giddings managed to win in a very close contest, Jones' strong showing demonstrated the growing divisions in the party and increasing dissatisfaction with Democratic leadership, and it proved that an independent with strong popular support could mount an effective campaign.

While Democrats had successfully regained the reins of power in Texas, their hold on the state was not as firm as it appeared at first glance. The lack of strong leadership on the state level, the division of the party into various groups with competing and often incompatible interests, and the prolonged economic difficulties faced by the state's farmers made the Democrats vulnerable.

Agrarian Dissent: Greenbackers, The Grange, and the Democratic Party

The most serious threat to the Democratic Party's control of state government was the continuing economic distress suffered by Texas farmers. The Panic of 1873 plunged the United States into a six-year depression and led to a general and steady decline in the price of cotton and other commercial agricultural products. Texas farmers associated declining agricultural prices with the deflationary effect of the Specie Resumption Act. The economic crisis in Texas was compounded by the drought which hit the state in 1878. The groups most effected by all of these problems were the new settlers who had poured into state in the late 1860s and 1870s and who were usually heavily in debt, and the numerous tenant farmers and sharecroppers who constituted much of the agricultural labor in Texas following the abolition of slavery.

To help farmers deal with these problems, three organizations surfaced in Texas in the mid 1870s. The Texas State Grange was organized in Dallas in October 1873; by 1875 it claimed 40,000 members with branches in all parts of the state. The Grange represented the first effort of Texas farmers to organize themselves for social, educational, and economic improvement. It exerted a considerable amount of influence in the 1875 constitutional convention, and continued to be a force of some significance in the Democratic Party through the mid-1880s. The Grange promoted public education (it was especially committed to the development of Texas A&M College), it helped win tax exemptions for farm products in 1879, and it agitated for effective regulation of railroad rates. The second organization, the Farmers' Alliance, was founded in Lampassas, Texas in 1875, primarily for the purpose of protecting farmers from unscrupulous land dealers. While the Alliance had over seven hundred local suballiances by 1885, and while it would exert a major influence on politics in Texas and throughout the South in the late 1880s, it offered no threat to the Democratic Party's power in the 1870s. The third farmer's organization was the National Greenback Party, which was established in the Midwest in 1874 in direct response to the passage of the Specie Resumption Act. In 1877, the Greenbackers spread into Texas where they set up a number of local clubs, especially in the northern part of the state, and a Greenback newspaper began publication in Austin.

In 1878 both the Grange and the Greenback Party played an active role in state politics. Although both organizations shared a commitment to improving the economic status of the farmer, they differed in their political tactics. In the elections in the fall of 1878 agricultural interests had an excellent opportunity to increase their influence in state politics as the Democratic Convention deadlocked in their efforts to nominate a candidate for Governor. The principal contenders for the position were Congressman and former Governor James W. Throckmorton and Governor Hubbard. Both men faced strong opposition. Critics accused Throckmorton of seeking the Governor's office as a stepping stone to the United States Senate, and questioned his involvement with the Texas and Pacific Railroad. Hubbard was also accused of conflict of interest in his dealings with the railroads and for other activities during his term as Governor. Both candidates were conservatives who pledged to reduce state expenses and the state debt. Neither candidate seriously addressed the concern of the farmers, although Throckmorton did favor expanding the supply of currency in order to raise farm prices. Dissatisfaction with both candidates prompted William W. Lange, Grandmaster of the Texas Grange, to enter the race. Although Lang withdrew after the fifth ballot, neither Hubbard nor Throckmorton was able to win the two-thirds majority necessary for nomination.

In an effort to defuse the heated debate over the nomination, the convention turned to a new candidate, Oran M. Roberts, Chief Justice of the Texas Supreme Court. Roberts, who had earned the affectionate title "Old Alcalde" during his tenure on the high bench, was a good choice as the party strove to heal the personality conflict between the Hubbard and Throckmorton factions. The "Old Alcalde" did not provide the strong leadership that the party clearly needed, but he was a capable administrator, and more importantly, because he lacked personal political ambition and therefore did not threaten any party faction, he was the ideal compromise candidate.

Although the nomination of Roberts represented a victory for the conservative wing of the party, the Democratic platform made an effort to appeal to discontented farmers by endorsing railroad regulation, an expanded currency, and the repeal of the Specie Resumption Act. However, the party did not go far enough on the currency issue to satisfy the Greenbackers, who called for the federal government to issue enough paper dollars (greenbacks) to cover the nation's treasury notes and bonded debts. Throughout the first half of 1878, enthusiasm for a separate Greenback ticket in Texas grew. The bitter struggle over the Democratic gubernatorial nomination convinced many that if the Greenbacks selected a strong and popular candidate, and if they could win the endorsement of Republicans, the Grange, and dissident Democrats, they would have a good chance to win the election.

Amid boisterous celebration and great enthusiasm, Greenbackers convened their state convention in Waco in August 1878. Most of the 482 delegates who assembled were farmers, although there were also lawyers, professional men, and laborers in attendance. Seventy of the delegates were blacks. The Greenback platform denounced both major political parties, and urged Americans to unite in a National Greenback Labor Party in order to "save businessmen from bankruptcy, the working class from starvation, the whole country from revolution, and the Nation from repudiation." More specifically they opposed the protective tariff, advocated the abolition of national banks, and called for the enactment of an income tax. On the state level, Greenbackers supported increased financial aid for public education, more protection for frontier settlements, lower taxes, and railroad regulation. The party's principal demand, the issuance of greenbacks as legal tender, was expected to be especially appealing to

Texas farmers, who suffered from declining agricultural prices and severe indebtedness. Greenbackers also hoped that their strong support of public education would attract blacks to the party. After approving their platform, the Greenback convention unanimously nominated William H. Hamman, a former Democrat, as their candidate for Governor.

The Texas Greenbackers based their 1878 campaign on winning the endorsement of blacks, Republicans, and the Grange. Initially, it appeared that their appeal for Republican support would be successful. Former Governor E. J. Davis and a majority of the Republican state executive committee announced their support for the Greenback ticket, and consequently did not nominate any Republican candidates for state office. However, a minority Republican faction, arguing that identification with the Greenbackers would isolate the party from the national Republican leadership (and their patronage), held their own convention and selected A. B. Norton for Governor and Richard Allen, the black Customs Collector for the Port of Houston, for Lieutenant Governor. The split within the Republican Party over whether or not to join the Greenback campaign, seriously jeopardized the Greenback chance for victory. Furthermore, Allen's presence on the Republican ticket undermined the effectiveness of the Greenback appeal for black votes. Although blacks played an active and very visible role in the Greenback campaign, on election day the black vote split, and Hamman carried only three of the fourteen counties with black majorities.

Even more disappointing was the failure of the Greenback Party to win Grange support. Fairly significant political and philosophical issues separated the two organizations, however. The Grange, for example, began as an organization which concentrated on helping their members achieve a fuller social life and deal with their economic problems. Although it became a fairly effective political pressure group, the Grange focused on non-political solutions to agrarian distress. They somewhat unrealistically urged farmers to abandon the single-crop commercial agriculture that had become widespread in the state following the Civil War, and return to simpler, more diversified agricultural production as a means to regain control over the marketing of their crops and achieve economic independence. The Greenback Party, of course, stressed political solutions to the problems of commercial agriculture, rather than the abandonment of that system of production.

Even when the Texas Grange became involved in politics, they were very reluctant to support third party movements. Memories of Reconstruction and Republican government were still too fresh, and the arguments for Democratic unity were difficult to resist. Furthermore, the Texas Grange believed that it had significant influence in both the state Democratic Party and the Legislature. Consequently, the Grange supported Democratic candidates in 1878. When Lang lost the Democratic nomination, he rejected suggestions that he run for Governor as an independent; instead he actively campaigned for Oran Roberts.

Roberts won the election easily with 158,933 votes. His opponents, Hamman with 55,002 votes and Horton with 23,402, made few inroads into areas of Democratic voting strength. Most Greenback votes came from counties in Northeast Texas where Republican and unionist sentiment was traditionally strong, and from Protestant workingclass neighborhoods in Galveston and Houston. Democrats also won four of the six Congressional races by large margins. In the Sixth District the incumbent, Gustavus Schleicher, who had alienated many of the farmers in his district by being the only Texas Congressman to vote for the Specie Resumption Act, faced a strong challenge from John Ireland, who entered the race as an independent. Although Ireland received support

Barker Texas History Center Photograph Collection

Governor Oran M. Roberts

from Anglo farmers, Greenbackers, and some Republicans, Schleicher managed to hold onto his seat. In the Fifth District, however, the popular Wash Jones, again running as an independent, put together a coalition of Greenbacks, blacks, Republicans and disaffected Democrats, and defeated the regular Democratic nominee, John Hancock.

Despite their poor showing in 1878, the Greenback Party remained intact in Texas and looked forward to the 1880 election with some optimism. The number of Greenback clubs in the state continued to grow and Texas Greenbackers played a prominent role in the national affairs of the party. However, the Greenback delegation in the state Legislature was too small to exert much influence in the lawmaking process, and although in Congress Jones took the Greenback position on the currency issue, he otherwise generally voted with the Texas Democratic delegation. Most importantly the Greenback party failed to win the support of the Grange, and lost the endorsement of the Davis wing of the Republican Party. In fact when the Republians rejected fusion with the Greenbacks and then nominated Davis for Governor in 1880, this ended any chance that the Greenbacks had for victory.

Governor Roberts dedicated his administration to cutting government expenses and reducing the $5,500,000 state debt that he had inherited from his predecessors. He achieved this by drastically cutting funds for public education and by increasing state revenue through the sale of state land. He authorized the sale of 5,000,000 acres of state land in order to pay the debt and at the same time reduce the tax burden on landowners. Roberts was sharply criticized for both of these measures. Lieutenant Governor Joseph D. Sayers challenged Robert's renomination, arguing that the Governor's financial policies were shortsighted and detrimental to the future growth of the state. However, Roberts' successfully reduced the taxes paid by farmers while reducing the state debt, an achievement that undermined his opponents' criticism and guaranteed his renomination.

In the general election in the Fall of 1880, Roberts received 166,101 votes, giving him victory by a substantial margin. Davis, the nominee of a reunified Republican Party, ran second with 64,382 votes, while the Greenback vote dropped to only 33,721. Following this rather sizeable set back, the Greenback Party would continue to operate in the state until 1884, but its effectiveness in Texas politics had ended. On the national level, the Greenbacker's appeal was weakened by the return of prosperity, while the implementation of the Specie Resumption Act in 1879 eliminated greenbacks as a major component in the currency debate. Instead, after 1880 the advocates of an expanded currency would shift their allegiance to free silver. In Texas, Roberts' land sales and tax reduction program provided immediate short-term economic benefits that overshadowed the more abstract appeal of greenbacks.

Although the Greenback movement failed to achieve its objectives in Texas, it did have a long-term impact on state politics. The fact that the Greenback Party received over 55,000 votes in 1878 illustrated a significant degree of dissatisfaction and impatience with the rather uninspired conservative leadership of the Democratic Party. Issues like funding for public education and the sale of public land would continue to divide Democrats during the 1880s. The party would find it increasingly difficult to balance the conflicting interests of their diverse constituency. Election results in the late 1870s also could be interpreted to indicate that the party's appeal was declining. While Richard Coke received 75.9 percent of the vote in 1876, Oran Roberts slipped to 67 percent in 1878 and 62.8 percent in 1880. Wash Jones' independent victory in the Fifth Congressional District demonstrated that if a popular candidate could unite various dissident elements, he would have a chance to break the hold that the conservative wing of the Democratic Party had on power in Texas.

Wash Jones and the Independent Challenge to the Democratic Party

During his second administration, Governor Roberts took few steps to answer the charges leveled at his administration by progressive elements in the Democratic Party. He did respond, at least in part, to criticism of his failure to provide adequately for public education. Under his direction in 1879 the state had established Prairie View Normal School and Sam Houston Normal Institute at Huntsville for the training of black and white public school teachers. In 1881, the University of Texas was established, completing a project which had been initially authorized by the legislature in 1858 and again by the Constitution of 1876. Otherwise Roberts remained firmly committed to the fiscal policies developed during his first administration. When he left office in 1883 he could point with pride to his success in implementing a "pay as you go" state budget, reducing expenditures, and improving the system of tax assessment and collection. Ad valorem taxes had been cut 40 percent, the state debt had been reduced by $1,000,000, and the state was operating with a budget surplus. On the other hand, thousands of acres of public land had been sold to speculators, social services had been significantly reduced, law enforcement efforts, especially on the frontier had been cut back, and despite the advances in higher education, public education was still poorly funded. When the governor's critics balanced his achievements against his shortcomings, they remained dissatisfied.

The decline of the Greenback Party and the continued weakness of the Republican Party caused progressive elements in Texas politics to seek a new alternative in their efforts to unseat conservative Democrats. In late 1881, Wash Jones provided this alternative when he announced that he was considering entering the race for Governor as

Barker Texas History Center Photograph Collection

Independent Congressman and gubernatorial candidate
George W. "Wash" Jones

an independent candidate in order to break the conservative hold on political power in Texas. This announcement, and the rumor that the national Republican administration would support Jones, sent a shock wave through the state, and triggered a serious effort to fuse all progressive groups in Texas into a single political movement. During the spring of 1882, dissident Democrats along with Republicans and Greenbackers held meetings around the state where they endorsed the concept of an independent ticket.

In late April 1882, Jones officially delcared his candidacy and the independent campaign began in earnest. Early developments in the campaign were promising as both the Republican Party and the Greenback Party endorsed Jones. At the Greenback state convention in June, the party approved a platform which accused the Democrats of failing to support public education, of selling state land to corporations and speculators rather than settlers, and of extravagance in the refinancing of state bonds. Then they adjourned without nominating a candidate. In late August Greenback leaders officially endorsed all independent candidates who supported their platform. The Republican Party adopted a platform which agreed with the Greenback planks on public education and land sales, and they accepted E. J. Davis' recommendation that they back independent candidates for state offices. Meanwhile, Republican President Chester A. Arthur had strengthened the Republican commitment to the independent movement by announcing his support for the Jones campaign and by removing from office two federal marshalls in Texas who had opposed fusion.

The Democrats would not have the advantage of the incumbency in the 1882 elections. After serving two terms Oran Roberts was ready to retire, and he resisted the persistent efforts of friends who tried to convince him to seek a third term. By the late spring, John Ireland was the only serious candidate for the party's nomination. Since he last sought the Governor's office four years earlier, Ireland had slightly moderated his political positions in an attempt to promote party unity. While he endorsed Robert's reduction of property taxes and the establishment of the University of Texas, he backed the demands of the progressive wing of the party for increasing the funding for public schools, aiding immigrants to Texas, and restricting land sales to actual settlers. Also he supported the state regulation of railroads, expanding the currency, lowering the tariff, and abolishing national banks. In the absence of any other serious contenders, the Democrats unanimously nominated Ireland and approved a platform reflecting his political views.

The gubernatorial contest got off to a dramatic start when the two candidates met in a face-to-face debate in Houston on September 2, 1882. In this setting Jones simply outshone Ireland. The latter, although intelligent and well-prepared for the encounter, was a tedious public speaker who could not match the appeal of his colorful and charismatic opponent. During the remainder of the campaign Ireland wisely avoided face-to-face confrontations. Jones, however, followed the Democrat into the conservative strongholds of East and North Central Texas, campaigning from community to community a day or so behind his opponent. This tactic enabled Jones to show off his colorful personality and eloquence, while emphasizing Ireland's rather dull campaign style. The Democrats tried to deflect the independent threat by warning voters that there was no real difference betwen Jones and the Republicans, and that a victory for the independents would reintroduce the excesses of radical Reconstruction. Jones, very conscious of the source of most of his support, appealed directly to Republican and Greenback voters. He denounced the Democrats for their record in Texas and their failures in Congress. He accused the party of vacilating on the currency issue and of failing to achieve a meaningful reduction in the tariff even though they had controlled the House of Representatives during the last session of Congress. He also condemned the conservative leadership of the Texas Democratic Party for their educational policy and their sale of public land.

The Congressional races in Texas were thrown into turmoil in 1882 by reapportionment. During the preceding decade, the population of Texas had grown from 818,579 to 1,591,749, and the state gained five additional Congressional seats. While there were intense contests among Democrats for nomination in ten of the eleven districts, only in the Seventh Congressional District did the party's nominee face strong opposition in the general election. In this race, Republican Thomas P. Ochiltree, a Confederate veteran and close associate of President Arthur, successfully challenged the Democrat, George P. Finlay of Galveston. The colorful, popular Ochiltree promised to use his connections in Washington to secure river and harbor improvements for Texas ports, and he promised tariff protection for sheep ranchers in South Texas. Ochiltree won with 55.6 percent of the vote, again indicating that a strong, popular candidate could defeat a Democrat.

In the governor's race, however, Wash Jones' popularity was not enough to defeat Ireland. Nevertheless, Jones made significant inroads against the Democrats, cutting their vote total to 59.5 percent. Jones did best in his old South Texas Congressional District and in areas of traditional Republican strength in the Hill Country, Northeast Texas, and along the Rio Grande where his personal popularity enabled him to run well ahead of Greenback, Republican, or independent Congressional candidates. Most of his support came from groups closely identified with the Greenback movement, especially tenant farmers, white Baptist and Methodist landowning farmers who were deeply in debt, and organized labor, and from the traditionally Republican black tenant farmers and laborers. However, he failed to expand beyond this base. Most other landowning farmers, as well as most ranchers, businessmen, German-Americans, and Mexican-Americans continued to vote for the Democrats.

Although he lost the election, the fact that Jones received a higher percentage of the vote than any other challenger since the end of Reconstruction stimulated interest in uniting independents, Greenbackers, and Republicans to create a new party. While interest in independent candidates remained high, no permanent coalition was created. After his loss in 1882 Jones maintained a low profile politically until early 1884 when he launched an attack on Governor Ireland for failing to deal effectively with the problems of western lands and fence cutting, and indicated that he might run for Governor again. At their state convention in 1884, the Greenback Party endorsed Jones even more strongly than they had two years earlier. Republican support was not as certain this time, however. The death of former Governor E. J. Davis in 1883 precipitated a struggle for party leadership that would divide Texas Republicans into black and "lily white" factions. The immediate heir to Davis was Norris Wright Cuney, a black labor organizer from Galveston. At the Republican state convention in Houston in September 1884 Cuney convinced a majority of the delegates to again endorse independent candidates for state offices. However, a minority faction which objected to Cuney's leadership and to the policy of fusion bolted from the convention. This faction held a separate meeting in Dallas where they nominated a Republican slate of candidates headed by A. B. Norton. Despite his failure to get the unified support of the Republican Party, Jones announced that he would run again as an independent candidate for Governor.

Although Ireland's handling of the land issue and the related problem of fence cutting generated a significant degree of dissatisfaction with his administration, the

Republican Leader Norris Wright Cuney

Governor retained control of his party, and in the absence of any well-organized opposition, he was renominated unanimously. Ireland's strongest potential opponent, State Senator Lawrence Sullivan "Sul" Ross, stayed out of the race, hoping that his patience would unify Democrats behind his candidacy in 1886.

The Governor's race did not generate the same level of excitement in the Fall of 1884 as it had two years earlier. In fact, Jones apparently recognizing the futility of his quest, did not campaign with the same vigor. He still attacked the Democratic administration, especially in the area of land policy, but this time he limited his campaigning to Central Texas. The results were not surprising. Ireland won with 210,534 votes to 88,230 for Jones and 24,485 for Norton. Jones received over 14,000 fewer votes than he had in 1882, while Ireland upped his share of the total to 65.1 percent. Democrats also recaptured the lone Republican Congressional seat when Representaive Ochiltree refused to run for reelection because he had been unable to deliver on his campaign promise to secure federal funds for river and harbor improvements along the Texas coast. Without a strong candidate like Ochiltree, the Republicans had no chance for victory.

There were several reasons for the poor showing of the independents in 1884. First, during a Presidential election year, appeals for party unity are particularly persuasive. In 1884 the Democrats, sensing that victory was at hand in the Presidential race, were less interested in Jones' independent candidacy. In addition, despite the efforts of Cuney and other state leaders, the Republican Party did not uniformly back fusion as they had in 1882. The existence of a Republican candidate on the ballot, especially since this was also a Presidential election, cut into Jones' Republican support. Finally, Jones never developed a strong campaign against Ireland, and failed to broaden the base of his support beyond what it was in 1882. Ireland, on the other hand, made a concerted effort to win the farm vote by including several agrarian demands in the Democratic platform, thus diminishing the difference between his party and the independents. Therefore, although there was open opposition to Ireland, even within the Democratic Party, Jones failed to capitalize on this discontent and channel it into the independent movement. Dissatisfied Democrats, on the whole, preferred to wait two years for the next elections rather than vote against their party.

The most dramatic aspect of the 1884 elections was Grover Cleveland's victory in the Presidential race. This fact, combined with the poor showing of independent candidates in Texas, led to the rapid demise of the independent movement. With a Democrat in the White House for the first time since the Civil War, and the expectation of increased patronage and influence on national policy, Greenbacks and independents drifted back into the Democratic Party. Among Republicans, Norris Wright Cuney's continued control deepened the split between the party mainstream and the lily-white faction.

Governor Ireland and the Democratic Party successfully survived Wash Jones and the independent challenge. Ireland served two terms as governor of Texas. Perhaps his most lasting achievement was to direct the construction of the new capitol building, a project which the legislature had initiated with the appropriation of 3,000,000 acres of land to cover construction costs during the Roberts administration. In addition, Ireland continued the fiscal conservatism of his predecessors, altering the process of tax collection in order to secure adequate funds for the treasury, and also upgrading the system of public education. On the other hand, Ireland faced considerably more difficulty in his efforts to handle long-standing problems related to the distribution of public land, and he and his party confronted new problems which seriously jeopardized Democratic unity.

Governor John Ireland and his staff in Houston in 1883. Governor Ireland is the dark-bearded man in the center of the photo who is not wearing a uniform.

Barker Texas History Center Photograph Collection

Democratic Unity Under Stress: Land Policy, Prohibition, and Railroad Regulation

Although the Democratic Party survived the challenges raised by the Greenback Party and Wash Jones' two independent campaigns, it did not achieve political unity. In the 1880s Democrats faced a succession of issues that intensified differences among the various constituencies which made up the party, and created new divisions.

The first of these issues was land policy. In one guise or another, land policy had been a major political issue in Texas since the days of the Republic. Land was the state's principal resource in the nineteenth century, and it was used to promote settlement and immigration, to promote railroad construction, to fund social programs like education, and to pay the state debt. The formulation of land policy was one of the most controversial elements in state politics, and particularly divisive within the Democratic Party. Farmers and ranchers, city dwellers and inhabitants of rural areas, proponents of public education, railroads, and speculators each had strong and often conflicting opinions on the disposition of the state's public lands.

Land policy resurfaced as a political issue in the late 1870s during the administration of Governor Oran Roberts. In his efforts to reduce the state debt, Roberts reduced funding for education and began the large scale sale of public lands. The Constitution of 1876 had set aside half of the state lands for public schools. In 1879, to fund the state debt and provide additional funds for education, Roberts called a special session of the Legislature and asked them to use public lands to solve the state's financial problems. The Legislature responded by enacting the "Fifty-Cent Law," which authorized the sale of unappropriaed public lands in unlimited amounts at a minimum price of fifty cents an acre, and the sale of school lands in tracts of up to 1,920 acres at a minimum price of one dollar an acre. Landowning farmers, who paid the largest share of state taxes, supported this policy which promised to pay the state debt and at the same time reduce *ad valorem* taxes. Potential speculators, of course, applauded the measure. On the other hand, Republicans and most urban Democrats accused Roberts of promoting speculation while making it difficult for actual settlers to acquire cheap land. Although Roberts was sensitive enough to the criticism that his budget cuts had undermined education to increase aid to public schools during his second term, he remained steadfast in his land policy despite widespread criticism of his land sales program.

The effectiveness and wisdom of Roberts' land policy is still debatable. On the negative side, the program did not raise enough revenue to retire even 20 percent of the state debt, while it opened the door to speculators, including many out-of-state and foreign investors, who purchased extensive tracts of land in West Texas. Critics also pointed out that new technology, including barbed wire and dry farming, made agriculture possible in the arid plains, but when settlers reached West Texas most of the land was already controlled by ranchers or speculators. In his own history of Texas, Roberts defended his policy with the observation that it was "better to sell the lands at a fair price and increase the school and other funds to help pay the public debt, thereby relieving the people from taxation, than to continue donating them to railroad companies...it was better to let the lands belong to individuals who would pay taxes upon them than for the government to continue to keep them for any purpose." Actually, not that much land was sold under Roberts' land law. Less than two million acres of state land were distributed under the provisions of the Fifty-Cent Law, while speculators in fact acquired many of their holdings by purchasing, at depressed prices, railroad land and land that the state had granted to veterans and widows.

When John Ireland became Governor in 1883, he responded to the critics of his predecessor's land policy by increasing the price of school land, by ending the practice of selling excessively large tracts of land, and by establishing a Land Board to oversee the administration of land policy. But Ireland faced a new and more perplexing problem related to fencing public lands and fence cutting. In the early 1880s, ranchers and some farmers began using barbed wire to fence in their land in West Texas. Frequently public land was fenced illegally, occasionally depriving others of access to water or to land that they owned which lay within the fenced area. When drought hit the western plains in 1883 many ranchers simply cut through the fences that blocked their access to the grazing land and water that they desperately needed. As fence cutting became widespread, tensions mounted and violence threatened to erupt, especially in those areas where farming and ranching overlapped. Because the actions of the fence cutters were generally quite popular in the western part of the state, Ireland had a difficult time suppressing them.

In 1884, the Governor called a special session of the Legislature to deal with the problem. In the ensuing debate, representatives from ranching areas defended fencing as a constitutional right, while farmers demanded that restrictions be placed on the practice of enclosing public lands and that gates be placed at regular intervals in all fences. Since a majority of the Legislators represented farming areas, these interests were reflected in the compromise that emerged from the deliberations in Austin. The fencing laws included a ban on the fencing of unowned public land, a requirement that gates be installed in fences every three miles, and a provision making fence cutting a felony. Although farmers achieved most of their demands, Wash Jones condemned the compromise as a surrender to the large landowners. A more serious flaw was the difficulty that the government had in enforcing the provisions of the fencing laws. Throughout the 1880s it was almost impossible for the state to convince West Texas juries (which were made up almost entirely of ranch hands) to convict a rancher accused of illegally enclosing public land.

The overall effect of the state's land policy did favor ranchers and large landowners who were able to acquire control over most of the available West Texas land at low cost. Farmers were unable to compete successfully for land and consequently the population growth in the western part of the state was small. In addition, despite Oran Roberts' hopes, the sale of public land did not produce the revenue that he had expected, nor did it solve the state's financial problems.

An even greater threat to Democratic unity was the debate over prohibition. As former Governor Roberts observed, this controversy generated the most exciting political conflict that Texas had seen in years and "stirred up society to its very foundations with a greater manifestation of universal feeling and interest than had ever occurred before in Texas."

The first step in the prohibitionist campaign to ban liquor from Texas came in 1875 at the Constitutional Convention when E. L. Dohoney managed to insert a local option provision into the state Constitution. When few Texas counties exercised their option to prohibit the sale of alcoholic beverages, Dohoney and others launched a campaign to bring before the voters a constitutional amendment to establish state-wide prohibition. During the early 1880s, support for this movement grew and the proponents of prohibition became both outspoken and well organized. In 1880 the Grange publicly aligned itself with the prohibitionists, and two years later the Greenback Party endorsed the move to push a prohibitionist amendment through the Legislature. Most importantly, 1882 also witnessed the emergence of two strong forces in the Texas prohibition campaign. First, the Women's Christian Temperance Union opened a chapter in Texas. The W.C.T.U. recruited the wives of a number of prominent Texans, including Senator Sam Bell Maxey, and became one of the most influential and fervent voices for prohibition. That same year J. B. Cranfill, editor of the *Gatesville Advocate*, joined the movement. Cranfill became one of the leaders of the prohibition campaign, while his newspaper developed into the most successful of the ten prohibitionist newspapers in the state.

In 1884, frustrated in their efforts to get a prohibition amendment through the Legislature, E. L. Dohoney helped organize a branch of the national Prohibition Party in Texas. Although Prohibition candidates attracted less than 4,000 votes in the general election, enthusiasm for the crusade against liquor continued to build. In the months following the 1884 elections, the opponents of prohibition began to organize in an effort to defeat the growing movement. In a debate with J. B. Cranfill, Congressman Roger Q. Mills condemned prohibition as a doctrine which was incompatible with the democratic principles of personal liberty and freedom, while Senator Richard Coke argued that prohibition would be detrimental to commerce and industry in Texas, and that it would encourage the development of a bootleg whiskey industry. In 1886 the state Democratic Convention, in an effort to defuse this potentially explosive issue, blocked efforts by Cranfill to place a resolution favorable to prohibition before the convention, and instead endorsed local option as a compromise solution to the problem that would allow each member of the party to work for his own point of view within his home county, without jeopardizing party unity.

The local option compromise did not satisfy the prohibitionists. Under Cranfill's leadership they convened a Prohibition Party state convention to prepare for the 1886 elections. The convention denounced both the Republican and Democratic parties for refusing to endorse a prohibition amendment for the state constitution, and nominated E. L. Dohoney for Governor. In the November elections Dohoney received only 19,186 votes, trailing both the Republican candidate and Sul Ross, the Democrat who won the election, by substantial margins.

Despite their poor showing in the 1886 election, prohibitionists achieved a major victory early the next year when the new Legislature gave in to mounting pressure and approved a prohibition amendment. The leadership of the Democratic Party finally allowed the amendment to pass in order to get the issue before the voters in a non-election year, when its impact on the party hopefully could be minimized. Also, by approving the amendment and turning the question over to the people of Texas, legislators of both major parties protected themselves from the charge that they were anti-prohibitionist. Since most politicians expected the amendment to fail, it seemed like a safe way to silence the prohibition movement.

The election on the prohibition amendment did not settle the issue, however. Passions, which reached explosive levels during the campaign, did not dissipate once the election was over. Both sides committed all of their resources to the battle. Prohibitionists held barbecues and mass meetings where their speakers addressed crowds of enthusiastic supporters. Leaders of the prohibition campaign included a large number of Baptist and Methodist ministers, the head of the Texas Grange, and prominent Democrats like Senator Sam Bell Maxey and Congressman John H. Reagan. The prohibition campaign also enjoyed a widespread support in the press, especially in Methodist and Baptist newspapers, and, of course, in J. B.

An 1887 political cartoon questioning the integrity of anti-prohibition Congressman Roger Q. Mills.

Cranfill's paper which moved to Waco and published daily during the late spring and summer of 1887. The prohibitionists based their arguments on morality, on a conviction that standards of virtue and humanity compelled all Texans to oppose liquor, and on a belief that there was a direct link between alcohol, crime, and poverty.

The anti-prohibitionists used campaign tactics similar to those of their opponents. Governor Ross, former Governers Oran Roberts and James W. Throckmorton, and Senator and former Governor Richard Coke headed a list of prominent Democrats who opposed prohibition. They based their appeal on concepts of individual freedom, and argued that voluntary personal temperance efforts were sufficient to prevent the abuse of alcohol. They also noted that prohibition would favor the rich, who could import liquor from out of state; injure Texas wine makers, brewers, and their employees; eliminate an important source of state tax revenue; and promote the activities of criminals and bootleggers. Congressman Roger Q. Mills made a strong appeal for black support by reminding black voters that they had not been allowed to purchase whiskey during slavery. Others attempted to link the prohibition movement with the old Know-Nothing Party, claiming that both were anti-foreign. The culmination of the anti-prohibition campaign came at a huge rally in Fort Worth ten days before the election when, in a dramatic climax to the day's events, State Treasurer F. R. Lubbock, addressing a crowd of about 40,000, read an anti-prohibition letter from former Confederate President Jefferson Davis.

On August 5, 1887 the voters of Texas overwhelmingly defeated the prohibition amendment by 220,627 to 129,270. Support for the amendment came primarily from North and Northwest Texas. White Methodists and Baptists tended to support the amendment, but only by a narrow margin. On the other hand blacks, Mexican-Americans, German-Americans, and most Republicans voted against it.

Democratic leaders had hoped that the election would end prohibitionist agitation and reunify the party. Instead, the campaign left deep wounds which continued to fester. Despite the extent of their defeat, a number of prohibition leaders claimed that they had lost because of voting irregularities and election fraud. At the Democratic state convention in 1888, a group of anti-prohibitionists, ignoring pleas for party unity, tried unsuccessfully to add a strong anti-prohibition plank to the party's platform. Despite efforts at conciliation made by most party leaders, the prohibition debate left the party deeply divided. Frustrated prohibitionists, convinced of the morality of their position, found defeat hard to accept. Many, blaming the failure of their cause on the opposition organized by the conservative leadership of the Democratic Party, had their ties to that party severely weakened. Since many prohibitionists came from those counties in Texas where prolonged agricultural distress was already causing farmers to organize politically, the prospects for future Democratic unity did not look too promising as the decade of the 1880s came to a close.

The third political issue to surface in Texas in the mid 1880s concerned railroad regulation. In the years following the Civil War, Texas developed a modern rail system, funded by generous grants of state aid and an influx of investment capital from the rest of the United States and from foreign investors. As a result, by 1890 the state contained over 8,600 miles of track, and a rail network which provided relatively inexpensive and fast transportation that facilitated the expansion of the agricultural frontier westward, helped transform agriculture from subsistence to commercial farming, and contributed to the development of the lumber industry and the beginning of manufacturing in the state's cities and towns.

While no one denied the benefits that resulted from the state's improved transportation system, many saw the railroads as a mixed blessing. By the early 1880s, complaints of railroad misdeeds were common in Texas. Rail rates discriminated against short haul shippers, often making it cheaper to purchase goods shipped into Texas from out of state than to buy comparable Texas products and pay the higher local freight charges. Also, farmers claimed that rates were not based on the cost of service, but on what the traffic would bear. Consequently, when harvests were good, freight charges increased and absorbed most of the farmers' profits. In addition, rebates, rate cutting, and kickbacks favored large shippers over small businessmen, thus undermining competiton and fostering monopoly. Texans also complained that the practice of granting free rail passes to legislators, tax assessors, and law enforcement officers unduly prejudiced state officials in favor of railroads. Finally, Texans protested that the capitalization and bonded indebtedness of the railroads usually exceeded actual construction costs, and that railroad management often took excessive profits while they allowed some rail lines to deteriorate due to the lack of adequate maintenance.

Even more disturbing was the fact that by 1881 Jay Gould and Collis P. Huntington had gained control over virtually all of the state's railroads. Gould dominated all railroads running east and north from Texas while Huntington's Southern Pacific monopolized traffic to the West Coast. In 1882, Gould and Huntington agreed to divide rail traffic in Texas between themselves, thus eliminating competition. This agreement was formalized three years later with the creation of the Texas Traffic Association, a pool which standardized shipping rates and divided traffic between the two major rail lines. While this agreement instituted a degree of self regulation which allowed the railroads to operate more efficiently and profitably, and to construct new lines into South and West Texas, it also provoked increasingly ardent criticism because of the widespread use of rebates and rate discrimination by the Association, and because of the deterioration of rail service in some parts of the state.

The campaign for state railroad regulation had begun in the mid 1870s. Under pressure from the Grange, the Texas Constitution of 1876 gave the Legislature the authority to regulate rail rates, required railroads which operated in Texas to maintain offices and records in the state, and it prohibited the consolidation of parallel or competing rail lines. When the state Legislature failed to enact legislation to implement these provisions, both the Grange and the Greenback Party began to agitate for more effective railroad regulation. The Grange, in particular, complained about the burden that high freight rates placed on the farmer, and denounced the "greedy mismanagement" of railroads and the efforts of railroad interests to control the Legislature and courts. They demanded a constitutional amendment to require the Legislature to control railroad fares and freight charges. Even some supporters of railroad interests, like former Governor James W. Throckmorton, endorsed the idea of a state commission to regulate railroads on the grounds that it would eliminate flagrant inequities in shipping charges and protect the railroads from damaging rate wars. On the other hand, in the mid-1870s, business groups, especially in rail centers like Houston, opposed railroad regulation because they feared that it would halt railroad expansion in the state. As a compromise in 1877 the Legislature passed a law establishing maximum freight rates at fifty centers per one hundred pounds per one hundred miles.

During the early 1880s, Jay Gould and other railroad executives lobbied energetically against state regulation, arguing that the Legislature did not have the expertise to set rail rates, and that they had no clear legal authority to do so. Gould personally visited Texas and warned that regulation by either the state or federal government would bring railroad construction to an immediate halt. Even though the Democratic platform in 1882 called for railroad regulation, and Governor Ireland asked the Legislature to consider a bill to regulate railroads in 1883, industry lobbiests successfully blocked meaningful action by the state government.

In the mid-1880s, the movement for railroad regulation received additional support. First, in 1885, business leaders in Houston and Galveston shifted their position and endorsed the demand for state regulation when they discovered that rate discrimination was causing cotton to be shipped out of Texas by rail instead of by sea through their ports. The next year, the Farmers' Alliance joined the cause while the Democrats reaffirmed their commitment. More dramatically, Texas Congressman John Reagan finally was victorious in his ten year quest to persuade Congress to enact federal regulation of interstate commerce. Reagan, backed by farmers and small businessmen who hoped for rate reductions, and by eastern railroads who saw federal regulation as an alternative to costly rate wars, achieved his objective with the creation of the Interstate Commerce Commission in 1887. Apparently railroad interests assumed that federal regulation would end efforts at state regulation. Instead, the Interstate Commerce Act intensified efforts to Texas to achieve effective regulation of *intrastate* rail traffic.

In 1887 and 1888 Texas Attorney General James Stephen Hogg began to strictly enforce existing state laws controlling railroad activity. He broke up Huntington and Gould's Texas Traffic Association with an anti-monopoly suit, enforced the provision that required railroads to keep offices in Texas, and threatened to revoke the charters of railroads that failed adequately to maintain their lines. Meanwhile, business groups in Houston, Galveston, and Fort Worth again called for a reduction in rail rates. With both business interests and farmers supporting railroad regulation, the Democratic Party finally took decisive action. In 1889 the Legislature again debated a bill to create a railroad commission with the authority to control railroad rates. When questions arose concerning the legal authority of the Legislature to delegate regulatory power to a commission, the Legislature, with broad based support from business and agrarian interests, passed a constitutional amendment establishing a state railroad commission. The voters of Texas would approve the amendment by a large majority in the general election in the Fall of 1890.

Again with the issue of railroad regulation, the conservative Democratic leadership had to balance conflicting interests for the sake of party unity. For a decade the farmers' desire for railroad regulation had been blocked by railroad lobbyists. In the mid-1880s, as business interests joined farmers in pressing for state action, the Legislature finally took action, approving a constitutional amendment and submitting it to the voters for approval. More significantly, the Democratic Party was changing. Increasing demand for social and economic reform, and growing discontent among elements of the Democratic coalition created pressures that the conservative party leadership would not avoid.

The Collapse of the Conservative Democratic Coalition

Through the early 1880s, conservative Democrats held onto the reigns of state government by maintaining a balance, albeit somewhat shaky, among the various interest groups and factions which made up the party, and by deflecting the several third party or independent movements which challenged them. In part, they achieved their success by incorporating just enough of the demands of their Greenback or independent opponents to keep the majority of their potential constituency within the

Democratic Party, while not alienating the conservative elements of their coalition. However, this balance was becoming increasingly difficult to maintain.

In the late 1880s, conservative Democrats confronted two problems that would severely challenge their ability to absorb dissident elements and yet maintain party unity. The first was a familiar problem, the continuing economic plight of the farmer. This crisis would lead to the emergence of the Farmers' Alliance as a major force in Texas politics. The second situation was new, the appearance of an industrial work force and the beginnings of an organized labor movement in the state. The development of railroads created this new class in Texas, as workers were needed first to build, then to operate the railroads, and then to work in the sawmills and other industries made possible by the new transportation network. The Knights of Labor was the principal organization in the early Texas labor movement. There was a link between the Farmers' Alliance and the Knights of Labor. Both perceived themselves as representatives of the working class, and both admitted as members all workers, agricultural and industrial. Also in the 1880s, both groups cooperated as they sought solutions to the problems of the working class.

Throughout the decade the farmers' economic situation deteriorated. As farmers, seeking the benefits of a cash economy, shifted from subsistence farming to commercial agriculture their problems intensified. The production of a cash crop, like cotton, promised a higher standard of living, but it also required machinery and more land, which increased the burden of debt and made the farmers more vulnerable to crop failures and declining agricultural prices. Debt and the unavailability of credit were particular problems for Texas farmers. Federal regulations prohibited national banks from granting loans using land as collateral, while Texas law did not permit the establishment of state banks. Farmers who needed financial assistance could borrow only from private banks, which charged high rates of interest, and generally were reluctant to loan money to farmers. As a result, crop failures and debt led to the growth of farm tenancy. Farmers also suffered from railroad rate discrimination and from a severe drought which hit Northwest Texas in 1886.

As we have seen, the Farmers' Alliance was established in Lampasas in 1875. However, the original organization collapsed as its members divided over whether to support the Greenback ticket in 1878. The next year the Alliance was reconstituted in Parker County as a secret, nonpolitical, self-help and benevolent association which grew slowly until the mid 1880s when the decline of the Grange and the final demise of the Greenback Party left it as the only organized spokesman for the farmer.

In 1886, at its state meeting in Cleburne, the Alliance announced that its principal objective was to end "the shameful abuses that the industrial classes are now suffering at the hands of arrogant capitalists and powerful corporations" and drew up a list of political demands which reflected the aspirations of both farmers and labor. They demanded the removal of fences from illegally enclosed land; the sale of school lands to settlers only; higher taxes on land owned by speculators; the regulation of railroads; the free coinage of gold and silver to expand the supply of currency, raise farm prices, and ease the burden of debt; and the creation of a national bureau of labor statistics. The Alliance then appointed a committee to present these demands to the Legislature. The political stance adopted at the Cleburne convention almost destroyed the Alliance. A faction, fearing that the organization was on the verge of creating an independent political party, formed an opposition Alliance. The following year, however, C. W. Macune succeeded in reunifying the Alliance, and under his very effective leadership the organization expanded throughout the South.

The Knights of Labor first organized in Texas in the early 1880s, especially in the larger towns and among railroad workers. While they were concerned about wages and working conditions, the principal objective of the Knights was to lay the foundation for a new social order where labor controlled the management of industry. They sought to achieve this end by developing workers' cooperatives. Despite this, the Knights enjoyed their greatest success when they concentrated on more pragmatic issues like the eight hour day and wages.

During the mid 1880s, there was growing friction between workers and the mostly absentee owners of railroads and some businesses. A short and successful strike against Jay Gould's railroad system in 1885 enhanced the reputation of the Knights and led to their rapid growth in the state. However, a strike on the Galveston docks failed when Norris Wright Cuney's black longshoremen opposed it, and the Knights lost a second, and this time violent, confrontation with Jay Gould in 1886. In this strike, the Great Southwest Strike, over nine thousand workers walked off their jobs. When a bloody battle erupted between strikers and strikebreakers in Fort Worth, Governor Ireland used the state militia to restore order and protect railroad property. Meanwhile, Gould's Texas and Pacific Railroad had passed into federal receivership, and federal judge ruled that the strikers against this line would be held in contempt of court if they did not return to work. The failure of the Great Southwest Strike, charges that the Knights of Labor were responsible for a terrorist bombing in Haymarket Square in Chicago in May 1886, and poor management led to the rapid decline of the Knights of Labor as a national labor union. However, the organization remained active in Texas through the mid 1890s. After the 1886 debacle, the Knights avoided strikes and concentrated on more peaceful tactics to achieve their objectives. In particular, they emphasized the need for political activity to deal with the anti-labor actions of the Governor and the courts.

Both the Knights of Labor and the Farmers' Alliance had an impact on the election of 1886. As Governor Ireland prepared to step down as the state's chief executive, five major candidates competed for the Democratic nomination. The major issues in the race included prohibition and the concerns of the farmer and worker, land policy, the regulation of railroads, and strikes. The Democratic convention selected Lawrence Sullivan "Sul" Ross, a former state Senator who took a moderate position on the issues. Ross supported the sale of public school lands to settlers only, and short term leasing of other state lands, but he avoided expressing a clear position on railroad regulation, strikes, and prohibition (although he was reputed to be an antiprohibitionist). Norris Wright Cuney managed to reunite the Republican Party following the split into black and white factions in 1884, largely over the question of fusion with Wash Jones' independent movement. Since fusion with the Prohibition Party was unpopular with both lily white and black Republicans, the party rallied behind a single Republican candidate, A. M. Cochran, for the first time since 1880. Despite Republican unity, Ross easily won the election, polling 278,776 votes to 65,236 for Cochran and 19,186 for the Prohibition candidate, E. L. Dohoney.

In the local elections the relative unity which the Democrats seemed to have achieved with the nomination of Ross was not very apparent. Instead, the Farmers' Alliance and other opposition groups organized a strong challenge for control of the Democratic Party in several counties. By and large the opposition groups chose to work within the party and even endorsed Ross' campaign for governor. At dozens of campaign picnics and rallies around the state, Knights of Labor and Alliance members agreed to remain within the Democratic Party and work for reform by taking over the machinery of that party rather than creating a third party movement. However, in a few counties "Human Parties" or "People's Parties" ran their

L. S. ROSS.

Barker Texas History Center Photograph Collection

Governor Lawrence Sullivan "Sul" Ross

own slate of candidates in order to challenge the banks, railroads, monopolies, and conservative Democrats. In the fall elections Democrats won every Congressional race. The new Legislature would contain only two Republicans and two independents, but at least twenty-six members, although nominally Democrats, identified with the Grange, the Alliance, or the Knights of Labor.

When the Legislature convened in early 1887 it faced a Senate election, a contest that would measure strength of the dissident forces within the Democratic Party. Although six candidates were mentioned at one time or another, and four actually received votes on the first ballot, the race ultimately narrowed to a contest between the incumbent, Samuel Bell Maxey, and Congressman John H. Reagan. Maxey, who had held this seat since 1875, and who represented the conservative leadership of the party, campaigned on his record, with support from the railroads, business interests, and ranchers. Congressman Reagan, riding a wave of popularity because of his successful advocacy of the Interstate Commerce Act, and his endorsement of free silver, drew much of his backing from the farming areas of the state. On the thirty-first ballot Reagan gained the advantage and unseated the incumbent. While Reagan and Maxey did not differ that dramatically in their political philosophies, the Congressman's victory symbolized the growing strength of the dissident challenge to conservative rule in Texas.

In 1887, as continued drought added to the troubles of farmers in West Texas, most political attention focused on the bitter campaign for prohibition which deepened divisions within the Democratic Party. Texas Democrats were also troubled by the apparent insensitivity of President Cleveland to the problems of agriculture. In May 1888, a convention of Alliance members, Knights of Labor, and a few ex-Greenbackers assembled in Waco to consider the situation that farmers faced. Although this group rejected the idea of a third party for the upcoming

Barker Texas History Center Photograph Collection

Congressman and Senator John H. Reagan

elections, they did prepare a list of political demands which included the abolition of national banks; a program of low interest federal loans for farmers issued in paper money using land as collateral; government ownership of transportation and communication systems; and the direct popular election of United States Senators, the President, and the Vice-President.

In July a second non-partisan meeting was held in Fort Worth. This time Democrats disillusioned with Ross' conservatism and a few Republicans joined discontented farmers. They endorsed the Waco platform but added demands for the free coinage of silver, immediate payment of the national debt, a graduated income tax, and compulsory arbitration of all labor disputes. More significantly, the Fort Worth convention decided to run a slate of candidates in the fall elections, and they selected Evan Jones, the President of the Texas Farmers' Alliance as their nominee for Governor. Two days later many of the same delegates reassembled in Fort Worth, organized a Texas branch of the Union Labor Party, and endorsed the candidates and platform of the earlier non-partisan convention. In August, however, the Farmers Alliance formally rejected any association with the Union Labor Party, and Jones refused their nomination. Union Labor Party officials then endorsed the Prohibition Party's gubernatorial candidate, Marion Martin. Throughout the campaign, the Alliance expressed concern about the deepening poverty of Texas farmers, but refused to oppose the Democrats or join any third party movement. The Union Labor Party actively pursued the black vote by nominating R. M. Humphrey, the organizer of the Colored Farmers' Alliance, for Congress. Consequently, Norris Wright Cuney and the majority of the Republican Party agreed to support Martin and the Union Labor Party. Once again, though, the Republicans split along racial lines with a significant minority refusing to follow Cuney's leadership. In the general election a number of these lily white Republicans voted for the Democratic ticket.

Governor Sul Ross won renomination with little opposition. The Democratic platform, however, encorporated many of the demands of the Alliance, including the abolition of national banks, the issuing of paper money, the reduction of the tariff, and the regulation of railroads and monopolies. This platform prevented a mass defection of farmers from the party, gained the endorsement of the Alliance, and enabled Ross to win reelection easily with 250,388 votes to only 98,447 for Martin. The Democrats again swept all of the state's Congressional seats, although a combination of dissident groups with strong prohibitionist backing ran a strong campaign in Roger Q. Mills' North Texas district. In legislative contests, People's Parties were organized in several counties, but reformers again achieved their greatest success electing Democratic candidates who openly identified with the Alliance or other dissident groups. As a result, farmers held the largest number of seats in the new Legislature than they had since the end of Reconstruction, including a clear majority in the State House of Representatives.

The Twenty-first Legislature, which convened in early 1889, was the first to assemble in the new capitol building. Perhaps reflecting their new surroundings, this Legislature directly confronted several of the problems that their predecessors had avoided, including the regulation of railroads and big business. In the process the conservative concept of limited government and the opposition to government regulation began to fade and seem less appropriate to the new economic and political realities facing the state.

The approval of a constitutional amendment creating a state railroad commission was one of the first achievements of the new Legislature. They also focused their attention on the concentration of corporate power and the anti-trust issue. Texas farmers protested about "cotton bagging"—the efforts of manufcturers to control the price of cotton—ranchers denounced the "beef combine" organized by the packing industry to control beef prices, and both groups condemned the activities of land speculators. The Texas Congressional delegation reflected these concerns by supporting moves on the national level that would lead to the Sherman Anti-Trust Act of 1890. On the state level, Attorney General James Stephen Hogg helped write a state anti-trust bill which outlawed business practices that were in restraint of trade, or which resulted in price fixing or the elimination of competition.

Organized labor did not achieve any clear victories in the Legislature, but they did intensify their political efforts in the late 1880s. Following their setbacks in 1886, the Knights of Labor focused on the campaign to establish the eight-hour day in Texas. In 1889 representatives from the Knights and other trade unions along with supporters from the Farmers' Alliance held an "Eight-Hour Day" convention in Dallas. The convention outlined a political action program which, in addition to calling for the eight-hour day, endorsed most of the reforms outlined at the Waco and Fort Worth meetings in 1888. More significantly, the convention established a State Federation of Labor to lobby for their goals.

The clearest indication of the changing direction of Texas politics was the nomination and election of James Stephen Hogg as governor in 1890. By the spring of 1889, the leading candidate to succeed the retiring Governor Ross was the popular and energetic Attorney General. Hogg won the endorsement of reform elements in Texas through his anti-trust and anti-railroad activities as the state's chief lawyer. Hogg was strongly backed by farmers and labor, but he also received the support of some business leaders and a number of young politicians who agreed with the candidate's concept of a more active government. Hogg skillfully used the issue of railroad regulation to win the support of businesses which suffered from the rate discrimination which tended to favor out-of-state competitors over Texas merchants, lumbermen, ranchers, and manufacturers. Although Jay Gould warned that railroad regulation would harm Texas economically, a fear which caused most urban newspapers to oppose Hogg, conservative elements in the party did not mount a strong campaign against him, and Hogg easily won the Democratic nomination.

Meanwhile the Republican split which had occurred in 1888 had not healed. Cuney still controlled the party machinery and arranged for the nomination of Webster Flanagan. The lily white faction held their own convention in an effort to "make war against Negro domination," but they could not find an acceptable gubernatorial candidate. With no serious third party or independent opposition, and facing a deeply divided Republican Party, Hogg did not have to appeal to the more radical elements in the Alliance. Running on a platform which opposed national banks and endorsed the railroad commission amendment, but which rejected other Alliance and labor programs, Hogg easily defeated his Republican opponent, 262,454 votes to 77,742. The Texas voters also approved the railroad commission by a margin of over one hundred thousand votes.

The election of James Stephen Hogg signaled the end of the conservative coalition which had dominated the Democratic Party and had held the reigns of government in the state since the mid 1870s. For almost a decade and a half the conservative concepts of limited government had controlled the state, largely by maintaining a balance among the diverse groups and interests which made up the Democratic Party. Potential dissent was either deflected by appeals to party unity, with a not too subtle reminder that the alternative to the Democrats was the hated Republican Party which had dominated the state during Reconstruction, or dissenters were won back to the party as Democrats encorporated the more moderate elements of the Greenback and independent programs into their party platforms. In the late 1880s, however, the persistent problems of farmers, the rise of organized labor, and the growth of railroads and big business created new issues that the conservative coalition that dominated the leadership of the Democratic Party could not resolve or deflect, or encorporte within its intellectual framework. This time, as the party absorbed demands for railroad regulation and anti-trust regulation, their commitment to limited government would not survive and conservatives in the party gave way to more moderate leaders like John Reagan and, of course, James Stephen Hogg. The direction of Texas politics in the 1890s and after would depend on the ability of men like Governor Hogg to organize a new coalition that would keep conservative business and railroad interests as well as reform elements like the Farmers' Alliance, organized labor, and the prohibitionists loyal to the Democratic Party.

Suggestions for Further Reading

The following material represents a selected list of some of the more readily available material on Texas politics in the late nineteenth century. For more detailed and extensive information the student will need to consult unpublished sources, especially dissertations and theses.

The best general history of Texas politics during this period is Alwyn Barr, *Reconstruction to Reform: Texas Politics, 1876-1906* (Austin, 1971). Also useful for any study of Texas politics are Ernest W. Winkler, ed. *Platforms of Political Parties in Texas* (Austin, 1916) and Walter Prescott Webb and Terrell Webb, eds., *The Handbook of Texas*, 2 Vols. (Austin, 1952). The latter work contains biographical sketches of most political figures active in Texas. Also interesting for its biographical information is Norman G. Kittrell, *Governors Who Have Been, and Other Public Men of Texas* (Houston, 1921). Classical works on Texas history, published in the late nineteenth and early twentieth centuries tend to be weak in interpretation but almost encyclopedic in the information that they provide. Especially interesting is Dudley G. Wooten, ed. *Comprehensive History of Texas, 1865-1897*, 2 Vols. (Dallas, 1889), which contains a lengthy section by Governor Oran M. Roberts, "The Political, Legislative, and Judicial History of Texas for its Fifty Years of Statehood, 1845-1895," in Ibid., Vol. II, pp. 7-329.

Two works on blacks in Texas, Alwyn Barr, *Black Texans: A History of Negroes in Texas, 1852-1871* (Austin, 1973) and especially Lawrence D. Rice, *The Negro in Texas, 1874-1900* (Baton Rouge, 1971), contain information about the Republican Party during the years following Reconstruction. Other materials on Republican politics include two works by Paul D. Casdorph, *The Republican Party in Texas, 1865-1965* (Austin, 1965) and "Norris Wright Cuney and Texas Republican Politics, 1883-96," *Southwestern Historical Quarterly*, LXVIII (April 1965).

Biographical studies of elected officials also provide insight into Texas politics during the gilded age. Among the most useful of this genre are Ben H. Procter's study of Congressman John H. Reagan, *Not Without Honor: The Life of John H. Reagan* (Austin, 1962), Louise Horton's *Samuel Bell Maxey: A Biography* (Austin, 1974), and Robert C. Cotner's *James Stephen Hogg: A Biography* (Austin, 1959).

The farmers and their organizations played a key role in nineteenth century Texas politics. The best material on this subject include two articles by Ralph A. Smith on the Grange and the Farmers' Alliance, "The Grange Movement in Texas, 1873-1900," *Southwestern Historical Quarterly* XLII (April, 1939) and "The Farmers' Alliance in Texas, 1875-1900," Ibid., XLVIII (January, 1945), and three works by Roscoe C. Martin on the Grange, the Greenback

Party, and the People's Party, "The Grange as a Political Factor in Texas," *Southwestern Social Science Quarterly*, VI (March, 1926), "The Greenback Party in Texas," *Southwestern Historical Quarterly* XXX (January, 1927), and *The People's Party in Texas: A Study in Third Party Politics* (Austin, 1933). A more general study which examines the economic conditions facing Texas farmers is Robert A. Calvert, "Nineteenth Century Farmers, Cotton, and Prosperity," *Southwestern Historical Quarterly* LXXIII (April, 1970). Two general works on farmers' organizations and their economic problems which place developments in Texas into a national perspective are Irwin Unger's *The Greenback Era: A Social and Political History of American Finance, 1865-1879* (Princeton, 1964), and John D. Hicks, *The Populist Revolt: A History of the Farmers' Alliance and the People's Party* (Minneaplis, 1931).

The emergence of organized labor in Texas is discussed in three pioneering works by Ruth A. Allen, *Chapters in the History of Organized Labor in Texas* (Austin, 1941), *The Great Southwestern Railroad Strike* (Austin, 1941), and *Texas Lumbering Workers: An Economic and Social Picture, 1870-1950* (Austin, 1961), and two more recent works by James V. Reese, "The Early History of Labor Organizations in Texas, 1838-1876," *Southwestern Historical Quarterly*, LXXII (July, 1968), and "The Evolution of an Early Texas Union: The Screwmen's Benevolent Association of Galveston, 1866-1891," Ibid., LXXV (October, 1971).

Several articles examine specific issues in Texas politics. Railroad development and railroad regulation are discussed in James R. Norvell, "The Railroad Commission of Texas: Its Origin and History," *Southwestern Historical Quarterly*, LXVIII (April, 1965), Robert L. Peterson, "Jay Gould and the Railroad Commission of Texas," Ibid., XLVII (January, 1955), and M. M. Crane, "Recollections of the Establishment of th Texas Railroad Commission," Ibid., L (April, 1947). Studies of land policy and land reform include A. S. Lange, *Financial History of the Public Lands in Texas* (Waco,

1932), Reuben McKitrick, *The Public Land System of Texas, 1823-1910* (Madison, Wisc., 1918), and Wayne Gard, "The Fence Cutters," *Southwestern Historical Quarterly*, LI (July, 1947). For first hand accounts of the nineteenth prohibition campaign see H. A. Ivey, *Rum on the Run in Texas: A Brief History of Prohibition in the Lone Star State* (Dallas, 1910), and two memoirs, J. B. Cranfill, *From Memory* (Nashville, 1937) and E. L. Dohoney, *An Average American* (Paris, Texas, 1907).